Finding Out About

ELECTIONS

Liberty of the Subject and "Freedom of Election"

John Priestley

Batsford Academic and Educational Ltd *London*

Contents

© John Priestley 1983

First published 1983

Typeset by Tek-Art Ltd, London SE20 and printed in Great Britain by
R.J. Acford Ltd
Chichester, Sussex
for the publishers
Batsford Academic and Educational Ltd,
an imprint of B.T. Batsford Ltd,
4 Fitzhardinge Street
London W1H 0AH

ISBN 0 7134 3666 2

ACKNOWLEDGMENTS

The author and publishers would like to thank the following for their kind permission to reproduce copyright illustrations: BBC Hulton Picture Library, frontispiece, pages 7, 11, 39, 40, 43; the Trustees of the British Museum, pages 9, 13, 14, 22, 27, 28; the Illustrated London News Picture Library, pages 31, 33 (top), 37; Liverpool Public Libraries, pages 5, 15, 35 (and cover); *Punch*, pages 19, 33 (bottom); Shrewsbury Local History Museum, pages 21, 24; the Trustees of Sir John Soane's Museum, page 17; Victoria and Albert Museum, page 25. The colour picture on the front cover is a Representation of the Election of Members of Parliament for Westminster, 1820 (Guildhall Library London/Bridgeman Art Library Ltd).

Introduction

When the first English Parliament met, in 1265, it consisted of two houses. Members of the House of Lords were not elected, but were chosen by the King; while members of the House of Commons were selected by the counties and boroughs which they represented. How they were selected was left to the county or borough. In 1430 an Act of Parliament laid down who could vote for county MPs, but nothing was said about boroughs and so each little town decided for itself on how its MPs should be selected. (Most towns had two.) In some places only the councillors had the vote; in others, the freemen (those men entitled to trade or work in the town) voted; while elsewhere it depended on the land you owned in the town or whether you had a house there. Each town had its own rules; in some, people who received charity had no vote.

At first, sending MPs to Parliament was unpopular, as townsmen had to pay their MPs wages and travel expenses. From the fifteenth century onwards, however, people realized that there could be advantages in being an MP — a landowner gained prestige, a lawyer could combine it with working in London, and it helped a person's career. Would-be MPs changed the system by offering not to claim wages and, at a later date, they even paid for town improvements in return for being elected.

Down to the end of the seventeenth century, population, wealth and MPs were mainly in the south and on the coast, but after the Industrial Revolution new towns grew up in the north, while people also moved from the countryside into the towns. Many of the former towns were little more than villages, in that their population had either fallen or remained static. Some large towns then had no MPs, while some small villages were represented in Parliament. The House of Commons was very unrepresentative in Scotland, fairly representative in Wales, while in England and Ireland it varied from place to place. In fact, Scotland had its own Parliament until 1707, and Ireland had one until 1801. Most MPs were elected without a contest, but when these did take place, they could be very exciting, with months of campaigning, weeks of voting, drunkenness, bribery, bands, processions and even riots. At that time, and until a century ago, all voters declared in public for whom they were voting.

This unrepresentative system was altered by the Reform Acts of 1832, 1867, 1884-85 and 1918. The Acts increased the number of voters and redistributed Parliamentary seats according to population. Other Acts, particularly the Ballot Act of 1872 and the Corrupt Practices Act of 1883, sought to prohibit bribery, fraud and intimidation, producing a system not unlike today's, except that no woman had a vote until 1918. More recent changes include lowering the voting age to 18 and altering the boundaries of constituencies to fit in with movements of population. In Britain, the candidate who gets the largest number of votes becomes the MP, even if he has less than half the total votes cast. Other systems of "proportional representation" try to share out seats among candidates according to the number of votes gained by each party.

A number of the examples in this book are taken from elections in Shrewsbury, where only freemen had the vote before 1832. Who used to have a vote in your town or village before 1832? Shrewsbury MPs in the early nineteenth century included a well-known general, General Lord Hill; a famous eccentric, Jack Mytton; and a future Prime Minister, Benjamin Disraeli. Has your town had famous MPs?

Useful Sources

1. ELECTIONS

Our best-known elections are the Parliamentary elections, which return MPs to Parliament at Westminster; but we also have local government elections and, in the past, a variety of local government officials were chosen in this way, including members of school boards, Poor Law guardians and even beadles. However, there are few records of such elections, compared to the information we have on Parliamentary elections. We should remember that electoral boundaries are changed from time to time, so the MP for a borough in 1800 may not represent exactly the same area as an MP elected for the same place today.

2. PEOPLE

(a) The librarian in the local history, or reference, library in your area will have books which include descriptions of local elections, and copies of your local newspapers.

(b) The archivist of your County Record Office will have documents, such as letters and financial records, which refer to elections.

(c) Your local librarian, if he or she has not got all the books you need to study an election, can get books for you from other libraries.

(d) Although MPs are busy people, your teacher might be able to arrange for him or her to visit your school or for you to visit the House of Commons.

3. VISUAL SOURCES

(a) The local museum may have election souvenirs in pottery, porcelain, glass or fabric, the last named being election "favours" and banners.

(b) The local museum or reference library may have pictures or photographs of local elections, as well as cartoons produced on behalf of rival candidates.

(c) *Debrett's Illustrated House of Commons* and similar books of biographical information about the more important people of you county, include photographs of local MPs. Biographies of famous MPs will include pictures of them.

(d) *The Catalogue of Political and Personal Satires in the Prints and Drawings Departmen of the British Museum* (11 volumes) can be found in large reference libraries only. From the index you may learn of prints referring to elections in your area, up to 1832.

4. WRITTEN SOURCES

PRIMARY SOURCES. These are original record which you may find useful in studying an election. Ask the librarians in the reference departments of large libraries, local history libraries, or county record offices if you can see any records they have about the elections in which you are interested. These records will be kept in the reserve collections, so you will have to wait a short time before they are brought out for you to see.

(a) *Local Newspapers.* These publish candidates' advertisements, describe elections and report speeches, the results of election and appeals, if a defeated candidate has appealed against a result. To avoid the political bias found in any one newspaper, you should try to see all the local papers that might cover the election in which you are interested – you will find the same incident reported very differently by papers with different politics.

(b) *Poll Books* These record, for contested elections, the votes cast by individual electors. The earliest known poll book dates from 1694 and the last from 1872, when the Ballot Act, passed in that year, made it impossible for anyone but the individual voter to know for whom he had voted. Between a third and a half of all contested elections between 1830 and 1872, particularly those in the smaller boroughs, are recorded in poll books.

(c) *Election Literature* This may include "squibs" (abusive attacks on political opponents mostly dating from before 1850), handbills, cartoons, posters and election addresses.

(d) *Manuscript Records* The papers of local landowning families, now held in record offices, often include correspondence and accounts that refer to Parliamentary elections, particularly when a member of the family in question was standing for Parliament.

(e) *Hansard* This record of Parliamentary events includes a full record of speeches made by MPs in Parliament.

SECONDARY SOURCES

These are books and magazine articles written by someone who has read the primary sources of information about elections.

(a) *The Victoria County History* If this important reference book for your county has reached the subject of elections, it will include useful information which you will not need to look up from other sources.

(b) *Local Histories* These often include descriptions of the better-known elections fought in your town or area. Your county historical society publications, and local magazines, may also include articles on elections and local MPs.

(c) *MPs' Biographies* Well-known local MPs sometimes wrote their autobiographies, or were the subject of biographies, which describe the elections in which they took part. The fullest biographical source is the *Dictionary of National Biography*. Obituaries of local MPs can also be found in the *Times* and in the local newspapers.

(d) *Other Reference Books* MPs in Parliament after 1832 are recorded in *Who's Who of British Members of Parliament* and the annual volumes of *Dod's and Vacher's Parliamentary Companions*. Some eighteenth-century MPs have biographies in books published by the History of Parliament Trust. MPs are also listed in *Whitaker's Almanack*.

(e) *General Reference Books* Other books on elections are listed on page 46.

This poll book refers to the Liverpool election of 1832. The initials on the right-hand side show for whom the voter in question voted. Which candidates get most votes from the voters named on this page? How many different occupations can you find amongst these voters? Are any of the voters ordinary working men? (Look for the description "labourer".) Why would you not find any women listed in a poll book?

Name	Occupation	Address		
M'Andrew Robert	merchant	Blackburne-place	E	T
M'Andrew W. B.	merchant	Islington	E	T
M'Ardle Peter	victualler	Gibraltar-row	E	T
M'Cabe Thomas	blockmaker	Great Crosshall-st.	S	D
M'Call James	victualler	Garden-street	E	T
M. Cammon John	merchant	Broad-green	S	D
M'Cann Edward	cordwainer	Lime-street	S	
M'Carter William		Park-lane	E	T
M'Cawley Patrick	teacher	Gill-street	E	T
M'Clellan Alexander	draper	Prices-street	L	T
M'Clelland William	blacksmith	Chadwick-street	S	D
M'Clumpha Adam	joiner	Key-street	E	T
M'Cluscy Patrick	warehouseman	Temple-lane	E	T
M'Conochie Edw.	mason	South Union-street	E	T
M'Coy Alexander	draper	New Milk-street	E	
M'Coy Alexander	grocer	Lower Frederick-st	E	T
M'Creery Daniel	labourer	Chadwick-street	S	T
M'Cracken William	merchant	Rodney-street	S	S
M'Crum Daniel	tailor	Bridgewater-street	S	D
M'Culla Samuel	coach maker	Gerard-street		
M'Culloch Edward	victualler	Lumber-street	E	S
M'Culloch John	surgeon	Crabtree-lane	L	T
M'Cullock Samuel	surgeon	Duke-street	E	T
M'Curdy John	draper	Great Crosshall-st.	E	T
M'Donald George	glass dealer	Robert-street	E	T
M'Dougall Duncan	merchant	Dingle	S	
M'Dowal John	gardener	Atherton-street	E	T
M'Dowell W. H.	printer	Finch-street	S	D
M'Gaa Ebenezer R.	spirit dealer	Salthouse-dock	E	T
M'Gaa John	bookseller	St. James's-street	E	T
M'Gee William	small ware dealer	Whitechapel	E	T
M'George Robert	draper	Byrom-street	E	T
M'George William	draper	Lime-street	E	T
M'Gill Thomas	merchant	Mount-pleasant	S	D
M'Gowan James	schoolmaster	Hope-street	E	T
M'Gowan Patrick	shipwright	Turner's-pl. St. Jas.	S	
M'Gready Edward	saddler	Dale-street	T	
M'Guffie John R.	druggist	Edmund-street	E	T
M'Guffie William	butcher	Berry-street	E	T
M'Intyre John	labourer	Mercer's-court	S	
M'Intyre Louis H.	book keeper	Seel-street	E	T
M'Intyre Peter	M.D.	Slater-street	E	T
M'Iver William	gentleman	Toxteth-park	S	D
M'Kay Hugh	provision dealer	Gerard-street	E	T
M'Kay James	tailor and draper	Chapel-street	E	T
M'Kee Charles	victualler	Spitalfields	E	T
M'Kellop John	blacksmith	Sparling-street	E	D
M'Kenzie John	merchant	Myrtle-street	E	S
M'Killop Daniel	ship smith	Robert-street North	S	D
M'Kune Kenneth	baker	Whitechapel	E	T
M'Laurin John	merchant	Kirkdale	E	T
M'Lean Allan	coffee merchant	Russell-street	E	T
M'Lean Hugh	labourer	Gascoyne-street	E	T
M'Lean James	flour dealer	Scotland-road	S	D

Constituencies

The first English Parliament to include representatives of the counties and boroughs was summoned in 1265. More boroughs later came to be represented until, by 1801, there were 465 MPs from England, 48 from Wales, 45 from Scotland and 100 from Ireland. Since then, changes, including Irish independence, have reduced the number of MPs in Parliament to the present total of 650. Of these, 523 are from England, 72 from Scotland, 38 from Wales and 17 from Northern Ireland.

Redistribution of seats, to try to ensure that, as far as possible, all MPs represent a similar number of voters, began in 1832 when representation was taken from small boroughs and given either to large towns or to county constituencies. However, these changes still left the small boroughs over-represented compared to the large towns. In 1861 both Leeds and Knaresborough had two MPs, although Leeds had 207,000 inhabitants and Knaresborough only 5,400. A new redistribution of seats in 1867 made matters more equal, although there was still room for more equality between constituencies.

By a new redistribution in 1884, most MPs represented a single-member constituency, although a few towns still had two MPs down to 1950. The old rule by which MPs represented either a county or a borough constituency, almost all of which had two MPs, was thus ended. County and borough constituencies had had different voter qualifications, and a county MP had had more prestige than a borough MP. Constituency boundaries are based today, as in the past, on local government boundaries, which alter from time to time as towns rise or fall in population.

The last Parliamentary Acts to alter the nature and boundaries of constituencies were passed in 1948-49, but every few years since then redistribution acts have been passed to change Parliamentary boundaries where necessary in order to ensure that all constituencies have roughly the same number of voters.

Can you say why some constituencies lose voters and others gain them?

What is the name of the Parliamentary constituency in which you live? What are its boundaries?

Who is your MP? Which party does he support? What was his majority at the last election?

This illustration from Pickwick Papers *by Charles* ▷
Dickens shows an imaginary election at an imaginary place called "Eatanswill" (study that name carefully and you will find a joke in it). You can find out the candidates' names from the banners. What signs of rough behaviour can you spot? How does this picture compare with the more serious view of an election on page 35?

The Franchise

The franchise is the right to vote in Parliamentary elections. Before the 1832 Reform Act this right depended, in the counties, on whether you owned land of sufficient value to qualify as a voter, and in boroughs on local custom. There were different kinds of borough, known as freeman, corporation, burgage, and scot and lot boroughs.

In freeman boroughs the general rule was that if you could practise a trade there, you also had a vote in the borough. Some freemen were quite poor people. In corporation boroughs, however, only council members could vote. All the Scottish borough constituencies were corporation boroughs.

The right to vote in burgage boroughs was attached to the ownership of plots of land called burgages. Some burgage boroughs had MPs but few, or even no, inhabitants. Old Sarum had no resident inhabitants, and so a tent had to be put up where the qualified voters could cast their votes.

The widest voting qualifications were in scot and lot, or potwalloper, boroughs, where to have the right to vote you must own your own house with its own door and fireplace and must not live off the poor rates.

Each borough had its own rules about voting and there were, in all, eighty-five different types of vote. It was not necessary to live in a borough to have a vote there and candidates in an election paid voters living elsewhere to come home to vote for them. Such "outvoters" could even outnumber the resident voters. In Scotland, landowners could create county voters by giving them temporary legal ownership of sufficient land for them to qualify as voters; while elsewhere men were often made freemen in order to qualify them as voters in a forthcoming election.

The Reform Act of 1832 gave the vote in boroughs to householders whose homes were rated at £10 a year or more, and thus created many new voters. In the counties after 1832, the old freeholder voters, with land worth £2 a year, were joined by others with similar qualifications, holding land in other ways besides freeholding, as well as by tenants who paid a rent of £50 a year. Those with the old voting qualifications kept the franchise for their lives, but all new voters in the boroughs had to be £10 householders – and only the middle classes owned houses of such a rating.

THE WORKING CLASS AND THE FRANCHISE

You can find out what the effect of the 1832 Act was on the working classes by reading the following extracts from politicians' speeches. In a speech on 23 April 1866 John Bright quoted what another MP had said in 1859:

> Ever since the Reform Act of 1832 the working people have been having less and less share in the representation. They had considerable representation before 1832 through the scot and lot voters and the freemen. They are gradually dying out.

Benjamin Disraeli, an MP of very different politics also said in April 1852:

> Under our old system, by the suffrages [votes] of the freemen, the political rights of the labourer were acknowledged . . . in fact we virtually terminated the political rights of labour with the class of freemen we destroyed . . . . I trace much of the discontent in this country . . . to this omission . . .

the ANTIQUITIES of MALMSBURY.

Another future Prime Minister, William Gladstone, made a speech before the 1867 Reform Act, saying:

> . . . of the total constituency of 282,000 in 1832 the proportion belonging to the working class was 87,000 or 31 per cent. They were now at the very outside not more than 26 per cent . . . the time has arrived when something ought to be done to increase their share in the elective franchise.

Why had the proportion of working people allowed to vote decreased by 1867?

This cartoon of 1792 makes fun of the electors of Malmesbury, where only members of the Town Council could vote. Four of the voters are holding horn books. Look up this word in a dictionary. Notice how the artist suggests that some Councillors cannot even read or write.

The 1867 Reform Act gave the vote to many working men in the boroughs and the 1884 Franchise Act did the same for county voters. No women had the vote in Britain until 1918, however. A more recent law have given the right to vote to all persons over 18.

MPs and Their Qualifications

Acts of Parliament lay down certain rules concerning MPs: for example, that an MP must be at least 21 and of British or Irish nationality. Some people are not allowed to become MPs; with certain exceptions, this is the case with peers, Anglican clergy from England and Ireland, Presbyterian ministers of the Church of Scotland, and Catholic priests. Many government employees are also disqualified from becoming MPs, including judges, civil servants, servicemen, police, some local government officers and certain other people paid by the state. Others disqualified to become MPs are those who are bankrupt, or of unsound mind, or convicted of treason or of election frauds. Before an elected candidate can officially become an MP, he or she has to swear, or affirm, certain declarations. In the last century, until the law was altered, these declarations or oaths could not be sworn by practising Catholics or Jews. Today, of course, both Catholics and Jews are often elected as MPs.

One can also say that there are some unofficial qualifications needed to become an MP. Very few non-party (Independent) candidates ever get elected, and so a would-be MP first needs to be selected as a candidate by the selection committee of a major party in a constituency. Even then, the candidate often has to fight a constituency which his or her party is unlikely to win, before being selected for a seat which the party can win. In the past, poor men found it hard to become MPs, as the payment of wages to MPs ceased in the seventeenth century and was not started again until 1911.

ADVANTAGES AND DISADVANTAGES OF A PROPERTY QUALIFICATION FOR MPs

To become an MP, until the qualification was abolished in 1858, one used to have to own a certain amount of land. Here are some of the arguments used by politicians when the abolition of this qualification was debated:

Mr Locke King. ". . . a statute requiring a property qualification . . . was first passed in the reign of Queen Anne with the avowed object of . . . admitting only persons connected with the landed interest [*landowners*] . . . . The qualification was fixed at £600 a year for counties and £300 a year for boroughs, and in both cases it was confined to [income from] real property [*land*] . . . since [then] personal property [*income from sources other than land*] has been substituted . . . . The practice of making false representations was, however, very common and he was told that after every general election there were usually from fifty to sixty cases in which persons declared themselves qualified who were not so . . . . This kind of legislation . . . encouraged members to make false declarations [to the House of Commons]."

Mr Bentinck, replying to Mr Locke King, said that "it was not correct that the object of the present law was to exclude all but those possessing land. The original object of the law . . . was to prevent persons being members of that house whose financial position was not such that they could devote their time exclusively to the business of the house . . . ."

Mr Walpole ". . . it was supposed that by requiring members to possess a certain income as a test of their eligibility, an amount of independence on their part might be secured. [A] second reason . . . was that it would prevent speculative candidates [*those candidates who stood without a chance of election*] . . . putting their opponents to unnecessary expense . . . . By . . . the present law we prevent able men with large professional incomes from taking their seats." (Hansard, 6 May 1858)

What arguments do the MPs speaking in the debate give (a) in favour of MPs having to own property? (b) against this?

Can you think of an argument for abolishing the property qualification that was not mentioned by the MPs quoted here?

This Punch *cartoon of the 1850s exaggerates the sale of seats in Parliament, by showing them openly on sale when, in fact, the offering of seats for sale had been made illegal in 1809. However, wealthy men could bribe patrons or voters in order to become MPs, whilst a poor man could not become an MP unless he had a patron. Some wealthy reformers bought seats in order to assist reform. Noblemen retained some influence over small boroughs, even after the 1832 Reform Act.*

Borough Patrons

Borough patrons were people in a position to select MPs for the House of Commons who would then obey their patron's wishes. Counties had too many voters for there to be control by a single patron, although an important landowner could be influential. Most boroughs, on the other hand, were small enough to be controlled by patrons, who nominated candidates who were almost certain to become MPs. The Government, through the Treasury, nominated some MPs, but many others were chosen by individual peers. Some peers could nominate several MPs, while others were able to nominate only one. By controlling votes in the House of Commons, a patron could gain promotion in the peerage or get into the Government, besides obtaining official positions, sinecures (jobs with a salary but no actual work), or service promotions for himself, his relatives, and his friends and servants.

THE MP AND HIS PATRON

An MP under patronage would resign if his patron wanted his seat for someone else, or if he differed from his patron on politics. MPs under patronage were not so influential in the House of Commons as independent MPs, especially those representing counties. Therefore, an ambitious MP with a patron would move, if he could, into a seat in Parliament which was not under the control of a patron. Francis Horner was a clever and ambitious MP who discovered some of the problems of being under the control of a patron in 1812:

A GOVERNMENT MINISTER PREPARES TO SUPPORT A CANDIDATE

Another person concerned with patronage was Sir Arthur Wellesley (later to become Duke of Wellington), when he was Secretary for Ireland in 1807. The following letter which he wrote shows us some of the factors involved in choosing a candidate for a seat in Parliament:

> I have made an arrangement respecting the borough of Downpatrick. This borough formerly belonged to Lord de Clifford, whose interest [*influence*] in it has lately fallen into the hands of Mr Rowley . . . and of Mr Croker, a gentleman who lately contested it against Lady Downshire. If Mr Croker will now stand he is to have the de Clifford interest, and he has proved to me that he can carry the election . . . . Under these circumstances, I have thought it advisable to encourage Mr Croker to persevere at Downpatrick. He has promised allegiance; and all that was required was a sum of fifteen hundred, or two thousand pounds, to enable him to carry on the contest, and I have by the Duke's [of Portland] advice promised to supply it. (Civil Correspondence of the Duke of Wellington, V. 42).

What do you think the money referred to in this letter would have been used to pay for? What would Mr Croker have to do in exchange for this support, to be useful to the Government?

> As to Parliament I have no seat because Lord Carrington, to whom I owed my last, has to provide for a nephew who has come of age since the last election, as well as for his son-in-law, who, being abroad, loses his seat for Hull; and because I have not money or popularity of my own to obtain a seat in a more regular and desirable way. (Francis Horner, *Memoirs*)

The Managers LAST KICK,
OR, THE DISTRUCTION OF THE
BOROUGHMONGERS.

Printed and Sold by J. QUICK, Bowling Green Lane, Clerkenwell, where Hawkers and Shopkeepers may be supplied.—PRICE ONE PENNY

A Whig view of the defeat in 1832 of those who controlled rotten boroughs. List as many rotten boroughs as you can find being driven out by Reform.

The King (William IV) was approved of by the Whig reformers, because he agreed to help get the Reform Bill passed by the House of Lords — you might like to find out how.

13

The Start of an Election

Here is an MP describing electioneering, in a letter to a friend:

> Think of me, the subject of a mob, who was scarce ever before in a mob, addressing them in the town-hall, riding at the head of two thousand people through such a town as Lynn, dining with above two hundred of them, amid bumpers, huzzas, songs and tobacco, and finishing with country dancing at a ball and six-penny whisk! I have borne it all cheerfully; . . . have been to hear misses play on the harpsichord, . . . Yet to do the folks justice, they are sensible, and reasonable, and civilized . . . (Horace Walpole, Letters (to George Montagu), 31 March 1761)

What feature of Horace Walpole's election would you still find in a modern election?

Canvassing meant that rich and influential candidates had to ask the poor for their votes — as in this humorous cartoon.

CANVASSING

Before an election the candidates "canvassed" the voters. Canvassing was the practice of candidates calling on voters to ask for their support. It is still a part of modern elections. A poem of 1841, called "The Election", listed some of the features of canvassing for the would-be MP.

> Grave talk with men how this poor empire thrives,
> The high-priced purchase from their prudent wives,
> The sympathising glance, the attentive ear,
> The shake-of-hand laboriously sincere,

How does a candidate try to win support in a modern election?

A Tory cartoon from Liverpool, a century ago, looking forward to the defeat of Smith, the Liberal candidate. You may be able to collect some interesting cartoons for yourselves before the next election — or try making some up. Today the political parties also put up posters and in some of these too, they draw attention to "mistakes" of their opponents.

COUNTING UP SUPPORTERS

From his canvass the candidate learnt how likely he was to be elected. Here is Lord Palmerston, later Prime Minister, describing his calculations about his candidature in a letter to his brother William:

July 17, 1826
... I knew my own strength, but not that of my opponents. I had obtained just before the poll began about 700 promises; the total number of voters was 1,800, of whom perhaps 1,300 might be expected to vote. This gave 2,600 votes, supposing each man voted for two candidates; and supposing that 200 people gave plumpers [*single votes to one candidate only*], it would leave 2,400 votes, which, between four candidates would be 600 apiece. I knew that out of my 700 promises ... I reckoned my casualties at 100 ... I knew, however, that Copley was strong and would probably poll more than his 600 ... and if, therefore, I polled 600 I might win ... (Delling and Bulwar, *Life of Lord Palmerston*, 1878)

Palmerston was standing for election as one of Cambridge University's two MPs. The result was that Copley with 771 and Palmerston with 631 votes were elected, while Bankes with 507 votes and Goulburn with 437 lost.

What matters would a would-be MP have to think about before standing for election nowadays? What does a candidate have to produce today before his name appears on a ballot paper as a candidate for election? Whose support does a modern candidate need before he can stand for election as the candidate of a political party in a constituency?

The Hustings and the Ballot

The picture on the front cover shows voters at the hustings in 1820, at the election of MPs for Westminster. At the hustings candidates were nominated for election and if there were no more candidates than there were seats to be filled, the election was an uncontested one and the MPs could be declared elected that same day. Uncontested elections were common in the past, but are very rare today. When there were more candidates than there were seats, then the election took place a few days after the nomination day. Unlike today, when election campaigns last a few weeks and voting takes place on a single day, past election campaigns could last for months and voting for one, two or three weeks. Until the Ballot Act was passed in 1872, everyone knew for whom an elector voted, as voting was in public. Since 1872, voters have marked their votes on ballot papers.

AN UNCONTESTED ELECTION

Here is a description of an uncontested Yorkshire county election in 1818, at which Lord Milton was the Whig candidate. The Whig party colours were buff and the "blue party" were the Tories. The letter was written by Francis Maude, an election agent for Lord Milton. He went to the hustings in York to vote for the nomination of Lord Milton.

> Wakefield June 25 1818
> Thursday Even
>
> My dear Lord,
>   I am happy to congratulate you on your being again returned a member for this County — I am just returned from York where we have had a most glorious day — I do not think I ever saw the Castle Yard fuller and a very decided majority were in our favour.
>   . . . You were . . . proposed by Sir L Wood and seconded by Geo. Strickland

THE HUSTINGS

A German visiting England described an election held in Westminster in 1782:

> The election was held in Covent Garden . . . . A temporary edifice, formed only of boards and wood nailed together, was erected . . . called the hustings [it was] filled with benches; and at one end . . . mats were laid, on which those who spoke to the people stood. In the area before the hustings immense multitudes of people were assembled . . . . To this tumultuous crowd, however, the speakers often bowed very low, and always addressed them by the title of "gentlemen" . . . .
> (C.P. Moritz, *Travels in England in 1782*, 1795)

> . . . . The blue party by hissing and clamour, riots upon the hustings and in the Yard, attempted to stop him — but he was supported by the majority and went on with great applause.
>   Mr Bethell proposed Sir Mark Sykes . . .
>   As no other candidate was proposed the Sheriff desired all those who were for the two put in nomination to hold up their hands — of course every hand was held up and you were both declared duly elected without there being any comparison between the friends [*supporters*] of each . . . . I was much pleased to see a large attendance of gentlem[en] of rank and consequence in the country in your interest . . .
>   Francis Maude
> (Wentworth Woodhouse MSS G.1.(20))

Can you suggest some reasons why this election was uncontested? Do you think the reasons were the popularity of the candidates, or their influence over their voters, or the money they had, or the greater popularity of their party policies? Or might there be some other reason?

A CONTESTED ELECTION

In a contested election, as in this example from Linlithgow in 1832, something like this would happen:

> The Sheriff called on the gentlemen present to propose and second the candidates. Sir William Baillie proposed Sir Alexander Hope, who was seconded by Mr Trotter.... Mr Gillon ... concluded by proposing Mr Hope Vere .... The nomination was ... seconded by Mr Hart. Sir Alexander Hope then addressed the electors .... Mr Hope Vere then came forward .... He concluded by urging the electors to send him to Parliament ...
> The Sheriff next called for a show of hands, which he declared to be in favour of Mr Hope Vere. Mr Dundas of Dundas then next demanded a poll on behalf of Sir Alexander Hope, which the Sheriff fixed for Wednesday and Thursday. (National Library of Scotland, Acc 5381, Box 13(2))

THE ELECTIONS

> Linlithgoshire — The poll for the elections for the County of Linlithgo closed on Thursday. The state of the votes at the closing of the poll was as follows:-
>
> For Sir Alex. Hope 267
> Mr Hope Vere 253
> Majority for Sir A. Hope 14
>
> (The *Scotsman*, 22 December 1832)

VOTING IN SECRET

The Ballot Act of 1872 altered the system of voting. Instead of voting in public, voters were now to vote on voting papers which they placed in ballot boxes. The *Times* reported:

> After an agitation of forty years the practice of secret voting is about to be adopted in England, or, more strictly, the liberty of concealing his vote is to be placed in the power of each elector ... those who say they are intimidated, or that their neighbours are intimidated, have established so popular a grievance that it must be respected. (The *Times*, 16 February 1872)

Who might have been intimidated before the passing of the Ballot Act? Can you think of anyone today who might prefer to keep their vote secret?

This famous picture by Hogarth in the mid-eighteenth century, shows the insane, the sick and the blind voting. It was important to get as many people to cast their votes for your candidate as you possibly could. Notice how public the voting is.

Why People Voted the Way They Did

Before an election, candidates made enquiries among voters and people of local importance, to see if they stood a chance of being elected. If they felt that they had no chance, they did not usually stand for election. The enquiries were made mostly among the most important landowners, whose tenants and relations would follow their lead and who well knew how their dependants voted, because all voting was in public. When constituencies had few voters, these voters were able to get favours from candidates and MPs, either bribes for themselves or official appointments for themselves or their relatives.

WORKING OUT HOW VOTERS IN SCOTLAND WILL VOTE IN 1788

In Scotland, in 1788, a Whig politician drew up a record, to which he added in later years, of all the 2,662 county voters for the 30 Scottish county seats in Parliament. He noted the names of each voter, the names of the persons whose lead the voters would follow, and a few personal details. At that date in Scotland county vote qualifications were attached to the ownership of land, and this could be transferred by legal means to any man, who would then vote as the original landowner wished. After the election the legal ownership was transferred back to the land-owner who had created votes up to a number that depended on the size of his estate.

Here is part of the 1788 information on the voters of Ayrshire. Each voter is given a number:

In this county there are a great many independent freeholders, and there are several individuals who from . . . their estates [and] family connections, have great weight.

One . . . is . . . the Earl of Eglinton, who has a very great estate, quite free of debt . . . . The Earl . . . was bound by a previous agreement to support . . . the Ministerial [Tory Government] candidate at [the] next election and he will certainly do this . . .

The Earl of Cassilis has also a great estate and many friends . . . [he] has few made [actual] votes but could make many . . .

Sir Adam Fergusson . . . has a great estate, many votes and some influence. He is an able man, and of a respectable character . . .

Votes of the Earl of Eglinton

. . .

20. Lieutenant William Ralston in Woodhill. The Earl's factor [estate agent].

. . .

Votes of Sir Adam Fergusson
60. Sir Adam Fergusson, Baronet. The Ministerial candidate . . .
61. Charles Fergusson. . . . Presumptive [future] heir of the last.

. . .

Votes of James Boswell
120. James Boswell of Auchinleck. The author of Johnson's life. . . . A very good estate. . . . Wishes to be a candidate for the county.

. . .

Individuals (Voters not following the lead of a landowner)
128. Thomas Miller, now Sir Thomas Miller, President of the Court of Session . . . . A very sensible worthy man. . . . Was made President by Mr Pitt, will support Sir Adam Fergusson.

. . .

161. William Cuningham of Lainshaw. Rich Glasgow merchant. Has a son at the Bar [a lawyer]. Wishes to get out his second son to India. Undeclared.

(*View of the Political State of Scotland . . . Confidential Report on the . . . 2,662 county voters in 1788*, ed. Sir Charles Elphinstone Adam, 1887)

What factors might affect the way voters cast their votes, according to the compiler of this list?

A humorous view of the various reasons why voters cast their votes as they did, from the first issue of Punch, *which appeared in 1841. Look carefully and you will find references to voters being bribed, or intimidated, or voting the same way as their fathers. Are any of the Scottish voters in the 1788 list expected to vote for similar reasons?*

Of course, people also voted for what the individual candidate had to offer — for instance, because he supported the abolition of slavery, or Parliamentary reform, or because he was a Radical.

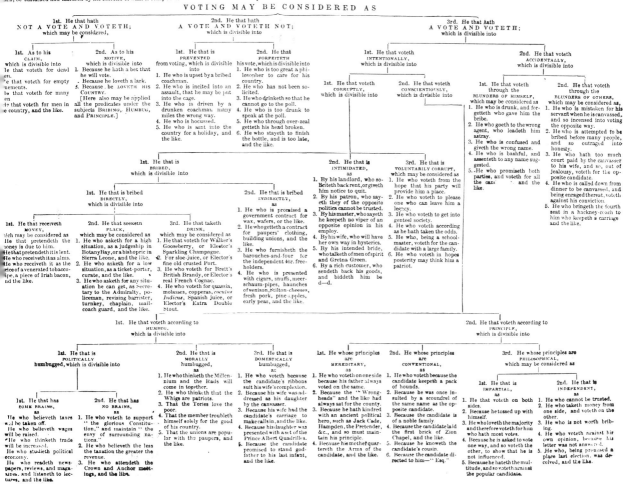

A SYNOPSIS OF VOTING, ARRANGED ACCORDING TO THE CATEGORIES OF "CANT."

~~~~~The Darker Side of Elections~~~~~

Election abuses disappeared slowly during the nineteenth century. You can read a good account of the old system, with open voting, in full swing, in the Eatanswill election chapter of Charles Dickens' *Pickwick Papers.* (See also the picture on page 7.) As late as the general election of 1880, nearly thirty election results were annulled because of fraud. Soon afterwards, however, the Corrupt Practices Act of 1883 was at last effective in making election bribery and fraud most unusual. It limited the amount spent on elections and the number of paid election workers, and so electioneering came to be carried out by unpaid volunteers, with a few paid workers, instead of by numerous paid election workers as in the past.

A ROUGH ELECTION AT SHREWSBURY, 1807

Here is how one election ended in Shrewsbury in 1807:

> In defiance . . . of the good and salutary advice given by the different candidates to their respective friends we are extremely sorry to state that a . . . riot . . . took place in the evening, and . . . most of the front, and some other windows of the Talbot Inn, where Mr Bennett and his friends dined, were demolished. (*Salopian Journal*, 27 May 1807)

BRIBERY AT A CORNISH ELECTION, 1819

A committee of the House of Commons in 1819 investigated an election held the previous year in Grampound in Cornwall. The committee questioned those involved in the election and, as a result of the investigation, Grampound lost its two seats in Parliament.

> Evidence of Alexander Lambe.
> How many voters are there for the borough of Grampound — I am not certain whether 58 or 60 . . . .
> Evidence of John Edwards.
> . . . I happened to be passing through Grampound . . . I met with one of the electors . . . I said, I supposed there could be no difficulty in taking the bribery oath . . . he believed there would be a great deal . . . he supposed very few more than three or four could safely take the bribery oath.
> Did Mr Allen's demanding the bribery oath cause a great sensation? — Very great.
> Did you see anything happen to Mr Allen [*a voter*] in consequence of his demand of the bribery oath? — . . . he withdrew from the hustings [in] the town hall . . . there was soon afterwards a report . . . that he had been assaulted . . . in the street . . . soon afterwards Allen returned . . . he appeared to have been exceedingly ill-treated . . .
> (House of Commons Select Committees, Vol. IV, 1819, 1853)

The bribery oath meant that the voters had to swear an oath that they had not taken bribes. If it could be proved that they had taken a bribe, they could be prosecuted.

Why do you think Mr Allen was attacked?

INTIMIDATION

Intimidation was another election evil. It could take various forms: a gentleman could threaten to withdraw his custom from a shopkeeper; a landlord could refuse to let a tenant continue to rent a house or farm. Here is an example of a different type of intimidation which existed even after the Ballot Act of 1872. Robertson was the Liberal candidate in the first election held in Shrewsbury after the passing of that Act.

Immediately after the contest on Tuesday last the usual reports of bribery, corruption and intimidation were pretty freely bandied about, and Mr Straight . . . hinted that unfair means had been used against him . . . a report that between 200 and 300 miners from the Brymbo Colliery Works . . . were brought to 'assist' in the election of the Liberal candidates. Suspiciously near as the Brymbo Colliery Works are to Mr Robertson's residence we sincerely hope that that gentleman will immediately repudiate . . . having any connection with the importation of this kind of electioneering crew into the town. (*Shrewsbury Chronicle*, 6 February 1874.)

Why do you think the bringing in of several hundred miners to "assist" was looked on as intimidation?

This side of the jug shows part of a print about the rotten borough of Bishop's Castle. The borough lost its MPs in 1832, in spite of the protests of its voters, who are represented here as birds saying: "You take away our lives when you take away the means whereby we live". Why would the rotten borough voters be so anxious to keep their right to elect MPs?

THE OLD ROTTEN TREE

Appeals

This unkind cartoon — look at the names of the councillors — refers to the dissatisfaction of the councillors of Boston, in Lincolnshire, with their new MP; but the petition they signed failed to unseat Sir Peter Burrell. Appeals against election results were judged in 1790 on party lines by the House of Commons, and strict justice was rarely the deciding factor. ▽

Once polling ended, the votes were counted and the result was announced, although, if the result was close, there might have to be a recount. If there was doubt about the fairness of the result, there could be an appeal.

1 Geo. Allspice 3 Thos. Tyson 5 John Buckles 7 Wm Bluster 9 Jno Whitebread 11 Moses Julep 13 Fras Parchment
2 Simon Primmer 4 John Squib 6 Thos Tinker 8 Brandy-Tipstaff 10 Thos Varguice 12 Thos Fussey 14 Honble Robt Cloggs

The ALDERMEN COMMON-COUNCIL &c of B———N in LINC———E signing the Petition on the 12th of Decbr 1790 against Sr PETER B———L whom they had just elected

DECIDING APPEALS AGAINST ELECTION RESULTS

Before 1868, the House of Commons tried appeals. Here are some of the arguments when it was decided that, in future, judges, and not the House of Commons, should try election appeals:

Mr Whitbread '. . . All that was wanted in the trial of an election petition was to ascertain a matter of fact . . . . That was not the province of a legislator [MP] but . . . the province of a judge . . .' (Hansard, 26 March 1868)

Mr Beresford Hope '. . . How could persons who were . . . political partizans go to the work . . . with dispassionate and judicial minds.' (Hansard, 21 May 1868)

Why were judges thought to be more suitable than MPs for trying election petitions?

THE JUDGES DECIDE AN ELECTION APPEAL AT EXETER, 1911

The *Times* reported on 5 April 1911:

Mr Justice Ridley and Mr Justice Channell yesterday began the hearing of the Exeter election petition in the Guildhall, Exeter.

Mr Dickens . . . explained that the original figures of the returning officer were:- Mr St. Maur 4,786: Mr Duke 4,782: net majority 4. There was a recount and the result was:- Mr St. Maur 4,782: Mr Duke 4,778. [8 votes objected to by both sides] were reserved for the consideration of the court [and] . . . about six others from the recount . . .

Individual votes were then scrutinized . . . consideration of the 14 papers left a majority of two votes for Mr St. Maur.

Counsel next proceeded to that part of the case referring to personation.

The case continued the next day:

Mr Foote KC, counsel for Mr St. Maur, took exception to . . . votes of a number of electors . . . [who] . . . were employed as agents, clerks [or] messengers . . . by Mr Duke.

Mr Duke now objected to 62 votes on the ground that the voters were employed at the election by Mr St. Maur for reward . . . . (The *Times*, 6 April 1911)

The hearing of the Exeter Election Petition . . . ended yesterday . . . proceeding were resumed . . . with the votes of each candidate standing at a total of 4,777. . . . Counsel for Mr Duke [*Mr Duke's lawyer*] . . . challenged the vote of a man who was said to have received payment . . . as [a] tally clerk and had voted for Mr St. Maur.

Their Lordships disallowed this vote . . . . .

After the decision of the Court declaring Mr Duke elected there were scenes of great excitement in the streets . . . Mr St. Maur . . . was enthusiastically cheered . . . . As the Judges left . . . the partizans of Mr Duke cheered them and those of Mr St. Maur hissed them. (The *Times*, 12 April 1911)

Who did the judges decide was properly elected as MP for Exeter? How long did they spend seeing if particular votes were valid?

Why were the votes of those who had been paid for working for an election candidate objected to in the appeal?

What do you think was the election fraud of personation mentioned in this report?

Election Relics

Quite a variety of objects survive that refer to past elections. Some of these were produced in the course of election campaigns, while others were made to commemorate election results. While an election campaign was in progress, posters, badges, cartoons, election addresses, election literature and even election ceramics were produced for the voters, and these can sometimes be seen today in museums, libraries and record offices.

Sometimes, when an election was over, a poll book (see page 5) was printed, to help in canvassing at the next election in the constituency; while medallions, pottery, porcelain and glass were sometimes used to commemorate election victories.

This election jug may be the first referring both to the local MP and to the party leaders of the two parties in 1790. The man who had the jug made had his name on it — Richard Biggs. Baker was the local MP. Can you guess what the figure after his name stands for? (Remember, he had just won an election.) He was a Whig, and the Whig leader was called Fox. Pitt was the name of the leader of the Tory Party. How are the party leaders' names used to make a slogan? ▽

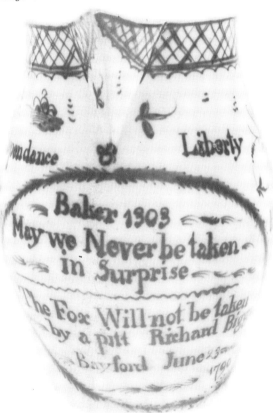

◁ *A jug made to commemorate an election victory. Which MP later became a Prime Minister? Can you discover the names of the other places he represented as an MP during his political career? (You will find one on page 33.)*

*Another version of the picture already seen on a jug
(page 21). This time it is on a handkerchief of 1831.
The branches of the tree and the birds' nests bear
the names of a number of rotten boroughs. The
Duke of Wellington, who opposed Reform, was
shown in cartoons with a huge nose. Can you find
him in the group propping up the tree?*

An Election of the 1820s

This section is the first of a series of descriptions of elections, all held in the same borough, Shrewsbury, during the nineteenth century. (See pages 30-1, 32-3, 34-5, 36-7, 38-9). Shrewsbury's MPs were either Whigs or Tories (later to be called Liberals or Conservatives). Like most boroughs, Shrewsbury had two MPs. Sometimes both belonged to the same party, though in other elections one MP from each party was elected. The franchise, or right to vote, was held in the 1820s by freemen burgesses (inhabitants with the right to work at a trade in the town) and these voters could either cast both the two votes to which they were entitled or a single vote, which was called a "plumper". If there were three candidates in an election, the voter who cast only a single vote assisted his candidate to win without helping either of his rivals.

THE LAST DAY OF POLLING

The poll was again resumed at ten o'clock on Thursday morning, for the purpose of admitting those burgesses who chose to vote to record their names, and of allowing a majority to be taken for Mr Slaney. Their candidate having resigned few of Mr Boycott's numerous unpolled voters came forward; on the part of Mr Slaney many respectable burgesses were polled, together with many others, whose votes, had there been a scrutiny, as on the former days, would have been rejected. The poll closed at one o'clock this day . . . (*Salopian Journal*, 21 June 1826)

Why do you think Mr Slaney's voters were admitted to vote on the last day without lawyers checking to see whether they were entitled to cast their votes? Can you list three differences between then and now in the ways in which elections are conducted?

THE CANDIDATES IN 1826

In 1826 there were three candidates, Slaney, Corbett and Boycott. The first of these was a Whig and the other two Tories. Elections in those days lasted for much longer than today, and all votes had to be given in public at the hustings. Voting was very slow and voters might have to swear that they were qualified to vote and that they had not been bribed. Lawyers for the candidates could challenge voters to prove their qualifications to vote. The 1826 election was described by the two local papers at that time, the *Shrewsbury Chronicle* (then a Whig paper) and the *Salopian* (Shropshire) *Journal* (a Tory paper).

Voting in the election lasted for five days and the voting figures, added together from day to day, were as follows:

	R.A. Slaney	Panton Corbett	Thomas Boycott
Saturday	69	129	68
Monday	142	257	144
Tuesday	235	438	239
Wednesday	275	505	276
Thursday	387	627	283

Slaney and Corbett were elected.

THE WINNERS CELEBRATE

The final ceremony of this election was the chairing of the elected MPs through the town:

The two members were seated in two chairs decorated with laurel and carried from the hall up Pride Hill to the Lion, where Mr Slaney remained. Mr Corbett's friends bore him to the Talbot. (*Shrewsbury Chronicle*, 14 June 1826)

What word would we now use in place of "friends" in this report?

Freedom & Purity of Election!!! Showing the Necessity of Reform in the Close Boroughs.

The cartoonist Cruikshank's view of the influence that could be exerted on voters by landlords in the 1820s. What has happened to the family carrying their belongings in the middle of the picture? Why are other families living in tents?

The Reform Act of 1832

Excitement over reforming Parliament lasted from 1830 until the unreformed Parliament passed an Act to reform itself two years later. These are the opening words of the Act:

Whereas it is expedient . . . for correcting . . . Abuses . . . to deprive many inconsiderable [*small*] Places of the Right of returning Members, to grant such Privilege to large, populous, and wealthy towns . . . , to extend the Elective Franchise . . . be it therefore enacted . . . That each of the Boroughs enumerated . . . Gatton, . . . Bossiney, Dunwich, . . . St Mawe's, . . . West Looe, . . . Camelford, . . . East Looe, . . . Winchelsea, . . . Tregoney, . . . Orford, . . . New Romney, . . . Bishop's Castle, . . . shall . . . cease to return any Member or Members to serve in Parliament . . . [*These places were all "rotten" boroughs, which had MPs but very few inhabitants or voters.*] . . . And be it enacted That each of the Places . . . Manchester, Birmingham, Leeds, . . . Sheffield, Sunderland . . . Wolverhampton, . . . Bolton, . . . Blackburn, . . . Halifax, . . . Oldham, Stockport, Stoke-upon-Trent, . . . shall . . . return Two Members to serve in Parliament . . .

Details of the "Elective Franchise" and its extension appear on pages 8-9. Which areas in particular have gained or lost MPs? Look at a large-scale map for an answer.

The "System" that "Works so Well"!! — or The Boroughmongers GRINDING Machine.

SHREWSBURY RECEIVES THE NEWS

Before it becomes an Act (or law) a Bill has to pass through three readings in the House of Commons and then through the House of Lords. Here is how news of the third reading of the Reform Bill was received in Shrewsbury:

The news reached this office . . . about five o'clock in the afternoon of Tuesday, of the third reading of the bill, and as soon as it became known . . . groups of persons assembled . . . mutually and enthusiastically congratulating each other . . . . . Towards ten o'clock at night a band of music was provided and . . . proceeded to meet the Wonder coach [*a local stage coach carrying the news*]. The crowd which had assembled . . . was amazing . . . meanwhile the Wonder approached, a blaze of torches was immediately raised . . . amidst the cheers of thousands . . . the procession safely reached the Lion Inn; and the joyful intelligence was confirmed to the people by the numbers of the Majority and Minority being proclaimed from the top of the coach . . . (*Shrewsbury Chronicle*, 8 June 1832)

In our last Journal we announced the third reading of the Reform Bill . . . the intelligence was received in Shrewsbury about five o'clock on Tuesday evening, . . . it was, however requisite that . . . the news should be received twice! in order that something like a fuss might be made . . . . Accordingly "a crowd" . . . including a band of ready-at-all-times musicians was put together, and, by the aid of a few gallons of ale & distributed to them . . . was kept moving about the streets from half past ten at night until about one o'clock . . . (*Salopian Journal*, 13 June 1832)

These are two very different accounts. It is easy to see which was the Whig paper supporting the Reform Bill. How does that paper convey popular support for the Bill?

This cartoon shows how wrong opponents of Reform were to say that the existing system worked "so well". For one thing, money from taxes ("Public Money") and government jobs went to the wrong people. The money was wasted on patrons and their friends, whose votes the government could buy with all the things you can see in the big bowl. You can find on the left of the cartoon the names of a lot of "rotten boroughs" — and under the building, a group of people who really needed public money spent on them. "St Stephen's" is another name for Parliament.

An Election of the 1850s

Here are some brief extracts from reports of the 1857 Shrewsbury election, which appeared in the local newspapers. One paper was Liberal and the other Conservative. These two parties were the only ones in Shrewsbury in 1857. In the election, Tomline and Slaney were the Liberal candidates and Huddleston and Phibbs the Conservative candidates.

ONE VIEW OF THE ELECTION

The nomination of candidates for the representation of this borough in Parliament took place on Friday, at the hustings erected in front of St. Chad's church . . . a large party of roughs planted themselves immediately in front of the hustings in order the more effectually to annoy the Conservative candidates . . . notwithstanding the repeated efforts of the Mayor to obtain a fair hearing for all.

The Poll
Opened on Saturday morning at eight o'clock and closed at four in the afternoon . . . . His Worship [*the Mayor*] declared the following as the result of the day's polling

Mr Tomline	706
Mr Slaney	695
Mr Huddleston	548
Major Phibbs	484

The successful candidates, Mr Tomline and Mr Slaney, afterwards addressed the electors . . . (*Eddowe's Shrewsbury Journal*, 1 April 1857)

A DIFFERENT VIEW

. . . Each candidate was escorted to the place of nomination by a large number of his friends and supporters . . . . The proceedings, though occasionally interrupted, were carried on with great good humour and notwithstanding the somewhat greater proportion of noise which prevailed on the Liberal side . . . each of the candidates had on the whole a pretty fair hearing.

Mr E. Hughes rose to second the nomination of Mr Huddleston, but he was received with such a storm of hisses, groans and cheers that it was impossible to hear him . . .

Mr A.S. Craig next rose, but it was some time before his voice could be heard above the groans and hisses with which he was assailed . . . he was . . . certain that Major Phibbs was a proper man to represent them . . .

. . . Shrewsbury election has closed. The cause of Liberalism has triumphed, despite the gross intimidation resorted to by the Tory party. (*Shrewsbury Chronicle*, 3 April 1857)

OCCUPATIONS OF THE VOTERS, 1857

Upon referring to the list of electors who polled it will be seen that about 500 professional men, and persons engaged in trade . . . excluding those who are employed, have voted for the Liberal candidates . . . on the other side we find about 350 professional gentlemen and others engaged in trade. (*Shrewsbury Chronicle*, 3 April 1857)

Why would it be impossible to write this paragraph in a newspaper today?

The 1857 election was for two MPs and the second MP elected was the same man who had been elected in 1826. Compare these accounts with the reports of the 1826 election on page 26. What two major changes have taken place in election methods since 1826? What were the politics of the *Shrewsbury Chronicle?*

The Successful Candidate; The Rejected Candidate. At this date elections were still lively and sometimes corrupt, as these Phiz cartoons from the Illustrated London News *of July 1852 show. They were noisy too. What evidence of that can you find in these pictures?*

The 1867 Reform Act was passed without arousing the political excitement that surrounded its 1832 predecessor. The 1867 Reform Act increased the number of electors from a little over one million to two million; borough electors more than doubled in numbers, while county voters increased by half. Most male workers in towns now had a vote. Redistribution took seats away from some smaller boroughs while giving further seats to Manchester, Liverpool, Birmingham and other large cities. The Act was the work of the Conservatives and was more democratic than had been expected.

Here are the comments of a Shrewsbury paper on the Act and on the election that took place the following year.

NEW VOTERS

The Reform Bill has escaped all the dangers which threatened it and our institutions rest thenceforth upon household and £10 lodger suffrages in the boroughs [*the vote had been given to those who owned their houses in boroughs, or were lodgers paying £10 rent a year*] and a £12 rating franchise in the counties [*county voters whose houses were rated at £12 a year or more*]. (*Shrewsbury Chronicle*, 16 August 1867)

THE 1868 ELECTION IN SHREWSBURY

In all the various phases the electioneering business of the borough has assumed there seems to have been an entire absence of many of the objectionable practices which have usually prevailed at contested elections. Treating there appears to have been none and, as far as appearances go at present there will be none. A greater amount of excitement, however, than prevailed this day (Monday) at the nomination has perhaps never been seen on any previous occasion in the borough; and this may have been expected from the large increase which has taken place in the number of electors under the new Reform Bill . . . . At the nomination . . . there was an enormous gathering . . . on the terrace by St. Chad's church, where the hustings were erected, and in the Quarry [*a local park*] below . . . (*Shrewsbury Chronicle*, 16 November 1868)

What do you think "treating" was and why was it thought to be objectionable?

The poll opened on Tuesday morning at eight o'clock, the votes being taken at polling places in different parts of the town — seven in all. Special constables were sworn in to preserve order, but their services were hardly required . . . there were but few drunken people about . . . walls and hoardings teemed with posters enjoining upon electors to 'poll early' . . .
    Declaration of the Poll
At four o'clock the electors began to assemble . . . as all were beginning to grow weary of the hubbub the Mayor rose and read the return which was as follows:-

868 Election

Clement (Liberal) 1840
Figgins (Conservative) 1751
Crawford (Liberal) 685
(*Shrewsbury Chronicle*, **20** November 1868)

What words are used here in place of "The election started" and "The result was"?

1047 voters voted for Clement and Figgins, 672 for Clement and Crawford, 2 for Crawford and Figgins; Figgins got 703 single votes, Clement 147 and Crawford 30. Compared to present-day elections, what is unusual about the way people voted? (Remember that Shrewsbury had two MPs at that date).

Why do you think Figgins got so many single votes?

A drawing from the Illustrated London News *of 28 November 1868 of the scene at a political meeting when Disraeli was nominated as the Conservative candidate for Aylesbury.*

A LEAP IN THE DARK.

In the 1867 Reform Act, Disraeli, then Chancellor of the Exchequer, had taken a major step towards making Britain more democratic. In this cartoon from Punch (3 August 1867), a frightened Britannia is jumping the high hedge of Parliamentary Reform. Why has her horse been given Disraeli's face, do you think? Why did some people regard the Act as a "leap in the dark"?

An Election of the 1870s

Two major changes had taken place in elections by the mid-1870s, one being the enlargement of the electorate in 1867, the other the introduction of the ballot in 1872. The extracts in this section describe Shrewsbury during the 1874 election, the first election after these changes.

ARRANGEMENTS FOR THE ELECTION

The following is a list of the booths provided for taking the poll . . .

Booth No. 1. Abbey Cemetery — For all persons entitled to vote in respect of property situate in the parish of Holy Cross and St. Giles . . .

Booth No. 2. Sutton Road. — For all persons entitled to vote in . . . Meole Brace . . . and the following portions of the parish of St. Julian, viz. Old Coleham, Sutton Road, Meole Road, and Belle Vue.

Booth No. 3. The Pound, Coleham. — For all persons entitled to vote in . . . the parish of St. Julian, viz. Longden Coleham, and the various Passages, Courts, and Squares . . . connected therewith, and Carline's Fields.

. . . . . .

Freemen — Every freeman . . . will be required to poll at the booth wherein his place of abode, as described on the register, may be.

(*Eddowe's Shrewsbury Journal*, 29 January 1874)

What important change has taken place since 1826 (page 26) in the method of deciding who was entitled to vote in Shrewsbury? Who were the two types of voter in Shrewsbury in 1874?

ELECTION DAY IN SHREWSBURY, 1874

The polling for the election of two members to represent this borough in Parliament took place yesterday . . . both parties used their most strenuous endeavours to bring their partisans [*supporters*] up to the poll . . . there was very little of that excitement that has hitherto characterised the elections for the borough . . . in the afternoon . . . The freemen and electors came up "few and far between" and the poll clerks had little difficulty in checking them off — and with the exception of a few drunken individuals . . . there was little to announce to a stranger that a great and important contest was going on . . .

At four of the clock the booths were closed, and the voters then made their way to the Market Square, expecting, as in old days before the Ballot was introduced, an official announcement . . . .

THE LIBERAL VICTORY

The double Liberal victory which was won . . . exactly reverses the position which the two political parties in the borough have held towards each other for several years past . . . . The Liberals, Radicals and Non-conformists [*Protestants, not members of the Church of England*] were surprisingly united . . . . The great advantage which Messrs Cotes and Robertson possessed over their opponents in being local men could hardly be overestimated . . . neither time nor opportunity was afforded the bulk of the

The crowd waited patiently until the return was posted up. The numbers were

Cotes. 1672
Robertson. 1561
Figgins. 1388
Straight 1328

. . . . . .

Our Defeat

Well, the election for this most ancient borough is over. Conservatism is for the present relegated to the shades. Radicalism reigns triumphant. . . . we must accept our defeat with as good grace as we can; . . .
(*Eddowe's Shrewsbury Journal*, 4 February 1874)

How has the reporting of elections and politics by a defeated side changed since the report of a defeat quoted on page 30? Can you work out to which party each candidate belonged?

PLIMSOLL AT THE HEAD OF THE POLL.

electors to test these candidates as to their political opinions on many of the most important questions of the day, while those questions which were likely to give rise to controversy were wisely omitted in their addresses. Then again the feud between Mr Robertson and the Non-conformists . . . was suddenly healed . . .
(*Shrewsbury Chronicle*, 6 February 1874)

When the Liberals had the support of the Non-conformists, what religious support was likely to be on the side of the Conservatives?

A Liberal view of an 1870s election in Liverpool, when the shipping reformer, Samuel Plimsoll, was the Liberal candidate. Plimsoll is at the top of the "pole", waving the flag. (Have you heard of the "Plimsoll line" which is put on ships? Find out about it — and you'll understand why sailors and their families voted for Plimsoll.)

Unlike the Reform Acts of 1832 and 1867, the reforms of 1884-85 did not combine in a single Act both an extension of voting rights and a redistribution of seats. Instead, an Act that extended the franchise was first passed, in 1884, adding two million voters to the electorate; and then a second Act, to redistribute seats, was passed in 1885. The household and lodger franchise, previously referring only to boroughs, was now extended to the counties. Many small boroughs now lost one or both members; some large boroughs gained members; and new boroughs were created. The old distinction between county and borough MPs disappeared, with all MPs now representing districts.

SHROPSHIRE LOSES HALF ITS MPs

. . . the Redistribution Bill . . . deals very hardly with Shropshire . . . the county and boroughs, instead of returning between them ten members, will, under the new Act, only return five, and thus half of the political interest of the district will be sacrificed . . . . Not satisfied with a reduction of our political importance by fifty per cent, the cut of the divisions of the county does not satisfy our revolutionary legislators, and . . . [the county will be carved] into four parts nearly equal [in population] . . . . We do not know whether the boundaries of the parliamentary borough of Shrewsbury will be interfered with by this division . . .
(*Shrewsbury Chronicle*, 5 December 1885)

Why did Shropshire lose half its MPs as a result of this Act, when other areas gained members?

A CONSERVATIVE VICTORY IN SHREWSBURY, 1885

By a majority of votes unparalleled in the annals of the borough Mr Watson and the Conservative cause triumphed . . . the Conservative party was thoroughly united . . . many moderate Liberals, alarmed at the confiscatory proposals of Mr Chamberlain, . . . on this occasion cast their lot with the Conservatives. Another helpful circumstance was that Mr Watson, a well known neighbour, had greater personal claims than the little known stranger who represented the Liberal party . . .

Shrewsbury Election
The Declaration of the Poll
Glorious Conservative Victory
The counting of the votes commenced on Friday morning at eight o'clock . . . and, at nine o'clock the poll was declared as follows:-

James Watson, Esq (C)	2244
Chas. Waring, Esq (R)	1512
Conservative Majority	732

A procession was formed which proceeded . . . to the Music Hall. . . . The procession was of a very motley character, and included aldermen, councillors, tradesmen, mechanics and a large number of working men . . . . Some bore flags and prominent in front a huge board was carried aloft bearing the state of the poll . . .
(*Shrewsbury Chronicle*, 4 December 1885)

The unsuccessful candidate is identified both as a Liberal and by the letter R, which stands for Radical,

1885 Election

the left wing of the Liberal party. Joseph Chamberlain, who is referred to, was President of the Board of Trade in the 1880-85 Liberal government, but later joined a Conservative government. While a Liberal Cabinet Minister, he had suggested that taxes should be raised. What three reasons does the *Shrewsbury Chronicle* give for the Conservative election victory in Shrewsbury in 1885?

The frontispiece of the Illustrated London News, *21 November 1885, shows Gladstone making one of the speeches which helped him to become Prime Minister four times. Notice how many people have come to listen to him, including women, who were not yet able to vote. He is speaking in the Free Church Assembly Hall at Edinburgh. Non-conformists tended to vote Liberal.*

An Election of the 1890s

Here are two rival notices for the 1892 election in Shrewsbury:

Gentlemen . . . Connected as I am with the Borough — having ties of family and of friendship and also owning property here — my personal interests are identical with yours. As a Conservative I absolutely refuse to entertain any proposal for legislation which may . . . impair the integrity [*give away parts*] of the Empire and I am in the heartiest accord . . . in resisting to the uttermost all attempts to destroy the Union of England and Ireland.

I am against the Disestablishment of the Church of England . . . and I wish to see all Nonconformists protected in the enjoyment of their freedom, rights and possessions . . .

A warm supporter of the cause of Temperance . . .

I am desirous of assisting in shortening the hours of labour . . .

H.D. Greene

Gentlemen . . . Having in my early life been intimately connected with the development of Railways and Industrial Enterprise in your ancient Borough . . .

As a Liberal and a firm supporter of Mr Gladstone, I believe that a Bill granting to Ireland the right and opportunity of managing her own affairs is due and just. . . . The Tories . . . promised to give the people of Ireland Local Government. They . . . have given them Coercion (*government by force*).

I ardently desire to promote every branch of Temperance Legislation . . .

The time has arrived when legislation is urgently needed to limit the hours of labour . . .

J. Brand Batten
(*Shrewsbury Chronicle*, 1 July 1892)

"Disestablishing the Church of England" meant ending its position as England's official church.

In 1886 the Liberal Government presented a Home Rule Bill to Parliament, to give Ireland its own Parliament and Government. Irish Home Rulers and Liberals supported this Bill which was defeated by the Conservatives (also called Unionists) and the Liberal Unionists, who wished to keep intact the union of Great Britain and Ireland.

Find out what temperance legislation was. On what subjects do the two candidates agree, and on what do they disagree?

ELECTION DAY IN SHREWSBURY, 1892

The electoral battle for the borough of Shrewsbury was fought and decided on Tuesday last . . . . Both candidates were astir early . . . . There was a very extensive display of political literature and both sides went in for a variety of cartoons . . . . Party colours were freely worn on both sides; Voters . . . ladies . . . children, and even dogs strutted about the streets gaily decorated with ribbons and rosettes!

Although the polling was, on the whole, conducted in very orderly fashion . . . there was one district, at least, that won for itself an exceptional notoriety — namely Coleham . . . . As the hour for the closing of the poll drew near, the feeling

The cover of this election address shows some of the better-known Liberal MPs of 1892. Can you find Gladstone? He was to become Prime Minister for the last time in 1894.

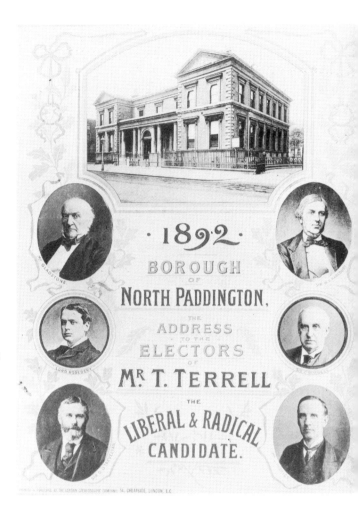

VOTERS IN SHREWSBURY

1841 Population of Shrewsbury: 18,245.
Votes in election: about 1,400.
1891 Population of Shrewsbury: 26,697.
Votes in 1892 election: 3,552.

What percentage of Shrewsbury's population voted in 1841? What percentage voted in 1892?

of this Home Rule faction rose excitedly and even angrily, and it was not without some personal risk that Unionist voters could venture to the polling booth . . . . It is to be hoped that this matter will be looked into . . . . Shortly after ten o'clock the result was declared as follows:

Greene (U) 1979
Batten (G). 1573
Majority 406

(*Shrewsbury Chronicle*, 1 July 1892)

Look at page 29 to see which side this newspaper used to support. What strikes you about the politics of this 1892 report? The letter G after Batten's name stands for the name of a well-known Liberal Prime Minister. Who was he?

Votes for Women

THE RIGHTS of WOMEN or the EFFECTS of FEMALE ENFRANCHISEMENT

*An election scene, 1853. This mid-Victorian cartoon
shows how the idea of votes for women was not
taken seriously. The women voters in this scene are
all supporting the handsome "Ladies' candidate".
What kind of man is the "Gentlemen's candidate"?*

THE WOMEN'S SUFFRAGE MOVEMENT

It was a long time before the idea of women voting
was taken seriously by men. One of the first men to
support the idea of votes for women was the writer
J.S. Mill who wrote in the 1860s:

> . . . there is a numerous and active society
> organised and managed by women, for the
> . . . object of obtaining the political
> franchise . . .
> . . . women require the suffrage, as their
> guarantee of just and equal consideration
> . . . their vocation for government has . . .
> become conspicuous, through the very
> few opportunities which have been given
> . . . (J.S. Mill, *The Subjection of Women*,
> 1869)

Can you name any successful women rulers of whom
Mill might have been thinking?

The women's suffrage movement grew slowly until
the years just before the First World War when they
were often in the news, especially when they used to
interrupt political meetings:

> . . . A vigorous attempt to interrupt the
> proceedings was made by a number of
> women . . . during the opening sentences
> of Mr Haldane's speech. Fifteen women
> and one man were ejected by the police.
> (The *Times*, 24 May 1909)

Mr Haldane was interrupted because he was a member
of the Liberal government which would not give
women the vote. What were the names given to
women supporters of the campaign for votes for
women?

WOMEN GAIN THE VOTE

Five years after the incident mentioned on page 40, the speaker, by then a member of the House of Lords, was a supporter of the idea of votes for women. Here are some of the arguments he used in a speech on the subject:

> . . . When you think of the extent to which men have changed the factory laws, mining laws, and the laws regulating the social environment in which they work, and when you contrast these changes with the slow changes in the field of women's work, you realise the effects of the absence of political influence in the ranks of women . . . . I deplore militancy. I think it has thrown back this cause. But at the same time it is inevitable that when a question of this kind becomes active that there should arise these things . . . . I believe that the right to vote is a right which will have to be conceded before long. (The *Times*, 6 May 1914)

The contribution of women to the war effort during the First World War, doing jobs previously held by men, was the principal factor in gaining women the vote. In 1918 the right to vote was given to all women aged 30 or over. In 1928 women got the vote at 21, the same age at which men were able to vote.

THE FIRST WOMAN MP

Here is an account of the election of the first woman MP:

> ### FIRST WOMAN MP
> ### 5,203 MAJORITY FOR
> ### LADY ASTOR
> . . . After the declaration of the poll Lady Astor addressed a large crowd from the balcony of the Conservative Club [in Plymouth]. She was presented with a silver cup from the women and children of the division [*constituency*] 'in honour of the return of the first lady MP'.
> . . . . . .
> ### A LADY IN THE HOUSE
> . . . The presence of a woman in the House of Commons as a member was almost inconceivable no further back than the years immediately preceding the Great War, so universal was the belief that . . . a member of Parliament should always be a man . . . . However all that has been changed by the Great War.
> (The *Times*, 29 November 1919)

See what you can discover about Lady Astor, the first woman to sit in the House of Commons as an MP. Nowadays, although half the voters are women, there are still only a few women MPs. Why do you think this is the case?

This cartoon supports the suffragettes, by pointing out the very different attitudes of Asquith, then the Liberal Prime Minister, towards the House of Lords and towards votes for women.

THE RIGHT DISHONOURABLE DOUBLE-FACE ASQUITH.

VOTES FOR WOMEN

Women's Social and Political Union.

4, Clement's Inn, London, W.C.

A.PATRIOT

Citizen Asq—th: " Down with privilege of birth—up with Democratic rule ! " | *Monseigneur Asq—th:* " The rights of government belong to the aristocrats by birth—men. No liberty or equality for women ! "

⸻ Twentieth-Century Elections ⸻

The twentieth century has seen some dramatic election triumphs, and disasters, experienced by all three major British political parties — the Conservative, Labour and Liberal parties — and the situation has altered considerably since the last of the three elections recorded in this section.

THE GENERAL ELECTION, 1910

In 1910 there was a Liberal government and there were many Liberal, and few Labour, MPs. The Liberal government was usually supported by the Irish Nationalist MPs and was opposed by the Conservative (Unionist) opposition.

State of parties at the dissolution [of Parliament]

Liberals	373 ⎫	
Labour Party	46 ⎬	502
Nationalists	83 ⎭	
Unionists	168	
TOTAL	670	
Ministerial Majority	334	

(The *Times*, 17 January 1910)

Analysis of the election returns
Members already returned

Liberals	274
Labour Members	40
Nationalists	72
Independent Nationalists	10
Unionists	271
TOTAL RETURNED	667
Ministerial Majority	125

(The *Times*, 2 February 1910)

THE GENERAL ELECTION, 1923

The 1923 election was the first in which more Labour than Liberal MPs were elected and, as a result, a Labour government was formed with Liberal support. The Labour party was taking over as the principal opposition to the Conservatives.

UNIONISTS IN THE MINORITY
A STALEMATE
PRIME MINISTER'S POSITION
THE CHOICE OF ALLIES

STRENGTH OF PARTIES

UNIONIST	254
LABOUR	192
LIBERAL	149
OTHERS	7
	602
Results to come	13
	615

With a few exceptions the results of the General Election are now known. The effect of them is to create a political situation which for dramatic interest has no counterpart in modern Parliamentary history . . . the situation which . . . must arise sooner or later under the three party system . . . no party is strong enough to carry on against the combined forces of the other two parties.
(The *Times*, 8 December 1923)

What event between 1910 and 1923 reduced the number of MPs and caused an important Parliamentary party to disappear from Parliament?

THE GENERAL ELECTION, 1951

By 1951 very few Liberal MPs were being elected to Parliament, although they still had a considerable number of votes. Almost all the MPs elected in 1951 were from either the Labour or the Conservative party.

MR CHURCHILL PRIME MINISTER
A SMALL MAJORITY FOR
CONSERVATIVES

. . .

STATE OF PARTIES

Conservatives and Associates	319
Labour	293
Liberal	5
Others	3
	670

The results in four constituencies remain to be declared.

PARTY SHARES OF THE POLL

Provisional figures show that over 82½ per cent of the total electorate voted. The aggregate votes cast in 616 divisions totalled 28,452,600. These were divided as follows:-

Labour	13,877,922
Conservative	13,665,595
Liberal	710,934
Others	198,149

Labour obtained 48.8 per cent and the Conservatives 48.1 per cent of the votes cast.

(The *Times*, 27 October 1951)

Compare the votes and the number of seats obtained by the Labour and Conservative parties. What is unusual about the result of the election? Can you suggest any reasons for the unusual result of the election?

Outside a polling station, 1955. By recording the voting card numbers of electors who have been to vote, parties can check which electors on their side have not voted and can then remind them to come along to vote for their party.

An Election of the 1970s

An election today is reported on TV and radio and in the press. Before the election you can read or hear the results of opinion polls; then you hear the early results and the way the election is going; and, a little later, you learn the final result which is analysed in the press.

SOME REPORTS ON THE 1979 GENERAL ELECTION

. . . the choice we have been offered at this election is, at best, a choice of evils. Labour's appeal has been to complacency. The labour leaders do not offer radical change, and they do not want it.

We have no faith in Callaghan and Healey, and no enthusiasm for Labour government. But it is the lesser of two evils. . . . (*Sheffield Free Press*, No. 30, May 1979)

For the first time I can remember the General Election has not been dominated by issues, but by the personalities of the two contestants for No. 10, Labour's Jim Callaghan and Tory Leader Margaret Thatcher. . . . (*Daily Record*, 1 May 1979)

Mrs Thatcher ducked away from a TV debate with Jim Callaghan because she maintained this wasn't a presidential style election. But in fact she was sent on a presidential-style tour culminating in a showbiz extravaganza in Wembley. She travelled 3000 miles on a calf-cuddling, tea-tasting, supermarket shopping, broom sweeping substitute for a political campaign. (*Daily Record*, 2 May 1979)

Four public opinion polls today support private assessments by both the Conservatives and Labour that Mrs Thatcher and the Tories will win today's General Election. The Conservatives believe they are poised for an overall majority of at least 30 . . . (*Daily Telegraph*, 3 May 1979)

The strong surge of Tory support for which she had been hoping materialised right across Southern England, but in the North swings were low and in Scotland it was Labour who gained ground.

The cruellest results of the night were for the Scottish National Party which after doubling its representation in the last decade was last night wiped off much of the map of Scotland.

The extraordinary divergence of the results region by region upset the computers . . . At one point the ITN computer was indicating a Tory majority of around 50 while the BBC computer was putting it in single figures. (The *Guardian*, 4 May 1979)

The registration form filled in by electors, in order to be registered to vote.

43 Majority for first woman Prime Minister

. . . . . .

State of the Parties

	Seats	Gains	Losses
Conservatives	339	61	6
Labour	268	11	51
Liberal	11	0	3
Plaid Cymru	2	0	1
Scots Nats	2	0	9
Others	13	2	4

Vote Totals and percentages

Conservative	13,697,753	(10,429,094)	43.9(35.7)
Labour	11,509,524	(11,406,768)	36.9(29.1)
Liberal	4,313,931	(5,346,704)	13.8(18.3)
SNP	504,259	(839,617)	1.6(2.9)
Plaid Cymru	132,544	(166,321)	0.4(0.6)
Nat Front	191,267	(114,415)	0.4(0.4)
Others	871,512	(887,588)	2.8(3.0)

(*Daily Telegraph*, 5 May 1979)

The figures given in brackets are the equivalent result from the previous (1974) General Election.

_____ AN UNFAIR ELECTORAL SYSTEM? _____

The Liberal vote of 4,313,931 was 13.8% of all the votes cast and a third of the vote cast for the Tories in their triumph; yet Liberals ended up with only 11 seats compared with the 339 Tory seats. It was the third highest Liberal vote since 1929.

If ever there was proof of an unfair electoral system this was it. If total votes really counted Liberals would be entitled to some 90 seats. (*Liberal News*, 8 May 1979)

Compare the election results of 1951, on pages 42-43, with those of 1974 and 1979. What major change has occurred to the number of votes gained by parties other than Conservatives and Labour?

What major alteration has happened in the way one hears about election results since the 1951 election?

Date List

1832 Representation of the People Act, 1832. (The First Reform Bill). Increased the number of people entitled to vote and redistributed seats in Parliament.

1867 Representation of the People Act, 1867. (The Second Reform Bill). Increased the number of people entitled to vote and redistributed seats in Parliament.

1872 Ballot Act, 1872. Replaced the system of declaring one's vote in public by secret voting, using ballot papers.

1883 Corrupt and Illegal Practices Prevention Act, 1883. Listed election crimes and the penalties these would attract. It also made clear the limits of expenditure on elections. It was a difficult act to evade and the penalties for election crimes made election agents keep within the law, instead of trying to win elections by bribery or fraud.

1884 Representation of the People Act, 1884. (This, and the following Act, are regarded as the Third Reform Bill). This Act further increased the number of people entitled to vote.

1885 Redistribution of Seats Act, 1885. This Act redistributed seats in Parliament.

1918 Representation of the People Act, 1918. This Act gave women the vote if they were aged 30 or over.

1918 Parliament (Qualification of Women) Act, 1918. Allowed women to sit in Parliament.

1928 Representation of the People (Equal Franchise) Act, 1928. Allowed women the vote at 21, the same age at which men had the vote.

1948 Representation of the People Act, 1948. Fixed Parliamentary boundaries and voting qualifications, abolishing university seats and the business vote.

1969 Representation of the People Act, 1969. Gave men and women the vote at 18.

Book List

For Adult Readers

Sir Charles Adam (ed.), *View of the Political State of Scotland. Confidential Report on the 2,662 county voters in 1788* (1887) (very detailed and of particular interest in Scotland)

H.J. Hanham, *The Reformed Electoral System in Great Britain 1832-1914* (Historical Association, 1968)

Sir Ivor Jennings, *Parliament* (Cambridge University Press, 1969) (much of interest on 19th and 20th century elections)

Sir Lewis Namier, *The Structure of Politics* (Macmillan, 1957)

J.E. Neale, *The Elizabethan House of Commons* (Cape, 1949)

H.G. Nicholas, To the Hustings. Election Scenes from English Fiction (1956)

C. O'Leary, *The Elimination of Corrupt Practices in British Elections* (1962)

E. Porritt, *The Unreformed House of Commons* (1903) (a full account of pre-1832 elections. Includes Scotland and Ireland)

J.R. Vincent, *Poll Books: How Victorians Voted* (Cambridge University Press, 1967) (what can be discovered from poll books about pre-1872 elections)

Organization of Political Parties in Britain (HMSO, 1983)

Parliamentary Elections in Britain (HMSO, 1982)

A series of books has also appeared on each general election from 1945 onwards. The general title is *The British General Election of* (date). The 1945 book was by R.B. McCallum and A. Readman, the 1950 one by H.G. Nicholas (publisher Frank Cass). Since then D. Butler has always been one of the authors, usually with a second author (publisher Macmillan).

For Young Readers

John L. Davies (ed.), *The Vote 1832-1928* (Jackdaw No. 16, 1965)

Frank E. Huggett, *The Battle for Reform 1815-1832* (Lutterworth, 1974)

Peter Lane, *Elections* (Batsford, 1973)

Iain Mclean, *Elections* (Longman, 1976)

allegiance   support for the wishes of a patron or for a cause.

Bribery Oath   a declaration, sworn by a voter, that he had not been bribed to give his vote. The Bribery Oath was not taken unless a voter asked that it should be asked for from all voters.

bumpers   drinks taken in honour of a candidate, party or party slogan.

burgage   a piece of land in a borough whose owner-ship gave the owner the right to vote. Such boroughs were known as "burgage boroughs".

burgesses   inhabitants of a borough with the right to work there.

canvassing   seeking the support of voters in a con-stituency by calling on them to ask for their votes in a forthcoming election.

chairing   the procession, after an election, when the victorious candidates were carried through the streets of the borough where the election had been held.

constituency   the area which returns one, or in the past two, MPs to Parliament.

contested elections   elections in which there was voting, as there were more candidates standing for election in the constituency than there were seats in that constituency.

corporation boroughs   boroughs in which only the members of the borough council had the right to vote in Parliamentary elections.

franchise   the right to vote. In the past this could depend on property, sex, custom or having a university degree. In elections today it depends on age and residence in a constituency.

freeholders   owners of land with the right to sell it if they wish without anyone else being involved.

freemen   men living in boroughs with the right to trade there. In some boroughs in the past only freemen had the vote.

hustings   the booths, or places, where voters declared to the voting clerks for which candidate they were voting in an election.

huzzas   cheers

interest   the influence of a patron in getting people to vote for his candidates in an election.

nomination   the ceremony at the hustings when candidates were proposed and seconded as stand-ing for election to Parliament.

open voting   voting in public at the hustings before the 1872 Ballot Act.

partisans   supporters of a political party (also known as friends).

patron   an MP under a patron had received his patron's support in order to be elected, and in return would vote in his patron's interests, and for the party he supported, in Parliament. Patrons were wealthy landowners whose tenants would vote for any candidate their landlord supported. Some MPs under patronage were relatives of their patron.

personation   the fraudulent practice of an imposter pretending to be a certain voter, presenting himself at the polling booth, and voting in his place before the real voter appeared to cast his vote.

plumpers   at elections for two MPs a voter casting only a single vote gave the candidate he supported an advantage over his opponents as, by not casting his second vote, he avoided giving the other can-didates any assistance. These single votes were called plumpers.

polling   voting.

Poor Law Guardians   officials who administered the workings of the Poor Law which provided official charity in the past.

Radicalism   the Radicals were the left wing of the Liberal party. Their principles were called Radicalism.

redistribution   the alteration of the boundaries of Parliamentary constituencies, to ensure, as far as possible, that all constituencies had approximately the same number of voters.

rotten boroughs   boroughs with very few voters, where the wealth or influence of a patron would always allow him to return to Parliament the candidate he wanted.

scot and lot (potwalloper)   an old qualification for voting in certain boroughs, where the ownership of a house with its own door and fireplace gave the owner the vote.

scrutiny   the practice of allowing lawyers to challenge the right to vote of a person who appeared at the hustings and wished to vote.

sheriff   the official of the county whose duty it was

to arrange the holding of county elections.

sixpenny whisk whist played for the low stakes of 6d for a hundred points.

suffrage the right to vote.

treating the practice of gaining support by giving free drinks to voters.

uncontested elections elections where there was no voting and the candidates were declared elected at the nomination ceremony, since the number of candidates standing for election was the same as the number of seats to be filled.

unpolled votes votes still to be cast in an election.

Unionists another name for Conservatives, especially in the period 1880-1922 when they supported the Union of Great Britain and Ireland. Those supporting Irish Independence were called Home Rulers or Nationalists.

Whigs supporters of the rights of Parliament, as opposed to those who supported the rights of the King. Supported by most of the big landowners, they were the ruling party for most of the eighteenth century. In the nineteenth century the Whigs became the Liberal party.

Index